AF337280

THE MIRAGE OF SHALE GAS

Thomas Porcher

THE MIRAGE OF SHALE GAS

Max Milo
ESSAIS-DOCUMENTS

©Max Milo Éditions

Collection Essais-Documents, Paris, 2018

www.maxmilo.com

ISBN : 978-2-31500-608-3

Introduction

Since François Hollande made a speech at the environmental conference of September 14th, 2012, France has been the first country to clearly reject shale gas and shale oil exploitation. The response was immediate: how could France, a country said to have the largest shale gas reserves in Europe, refuse to use them, while on a global level all countries seem willing to follow the American model?

Experts such as Claude Allègre, consultants, clubs, foundations, leaders, journalists, politicians, oil company lobbyists – all have published columns in favour of shale gas, putting forth arguments such as energy independence, lower gas prices, tax revenues and job creation that would result from exploitation. Despite opinion polls being largely opposed to shale gas, some have even argued that the French were incapable of recognizing the importance of the issues at stake and that the debate should remain primarily a conversation between professionals and experts, far from the irrational, emotional reactions of ill-informed individuals. Indeed, for shale gas supporters, the debate has not been led appropriately, firstly because of blackmail by environmentalists but also, and mainly, because of a "French syndrome", stasis, which according to some has crystallised all of France's ills for 30 years: the welfare state, the rejection of progress and the will to avoid the structural change that is needed to adapt France to globalisation. Even the Gallois report on competitiveness commissioned by the Prime Minister does not completely close the door on shale gas, and recommends further research on how to improve extraction conditions.

Currently, the debate opposes the supporters of exploitation on the one hand, who emphasise the economic gains resulting from shale gas production, and, on the other hand, environmentalists who advocate the precautionary principle regarding the extraction technique that is used: hydraulic fracturing – a technique designed to inject large quantities of water (12 to 30 millions of liters) mixed with chemical fluids. From the pro-exploitation side, we hear that France, which is going through a severe economic crisis, cannot do without the benefits in terms of job creation, production and purchasing power which would derive from shale gas exploitation. The environmentalists on the other hand focus on the groundwater pollution risks that could be generated by hydraulic fracturing. The reduction of the debate to a balance between economic gains and environmental costs is also time-related since, respectively, gains would supposedly be short-term, as opposed to long-term risks. Yet, in fact, the debate as presented to the public is biased, since it is based on the assumption that shale gas exploitation would necessarily impact positively on the economy. Which is far from being certain. Therefore I mainly propose to refocus the debate on one question: would there be economic gains for the country's population if France exploited its shale gas reserves?

The decision to set aside environmental issues does not mean that they deserve a second-rate analysis, but that they can be settled with certainty: no one today can claim that hydraulic fracturing does not pose any risks to the environment. On the contrary, economic gains can be assessed more seriously than they have been until now, which is the purpose of this text: to provide citizens with information, to present them with a more accurate framework concerning the American example and to take into account the judicial and economic specificities of the French system, in order for everyone to be able to comprehend who would truly benefit from shale gas exploitation.

THE MYTH OF THE TREASURE BURIED IN THE GROUND

In some media sources, all references to shale gas are followed by the story of a couple from Pennsylvania, both farmers, who became rich after accepting for a well to be drilled in their garden. Actually, in the United States, if the owner of a piece of land with shale gas reserves underground accepts the installation of a well, he or she receives financial compensation from the exploiting company, firstly beforehand, to finance the installation of the well, then through annual royalties on gas production. For the landowner, this can result in additional tens of thousands of dollars. However, contrary to the USA where underground resources belong to individual owners, in France they belong to the State. This means that if gas reserves were to be exploited, landowners would receive little money, if any. Even worse, if exploitable gas is found, there is nothing to prevent the State from accepting for a well to be drilled near residential areas. In that case, the residents of such areas near the borehole have to suffer the nuisance without deriving any benefits from the exploitation.

Even if the State is the sole beneficiary of the royalties paid by gas companies, some would argue that in the current context, public authorities cannot do without such tax revenue; however we will see later on that the mining code does not allow the State to receive expensive royalties either. In the case of France, what is worse is that inhabitants of areas rich in shale gas run the risk of becoming poorer. A report by the NBER[1] (National Bureau of Economic Research) shows the impact of shale gas development on real estate value in Pennsylvania. It turns out that the value of a property with a borehole in the garden rises by 10,7%, which probably reflects the additional benefits deriving from company royalties. As we have seen, this scenario is impossible in France since underground resources do not belong to the owner but to the State. Conversely, the study shows that within a 2000-metre radius around a borehole, the price of real estate decreases by up to 24% of its value. This decrease can be explained by the nuisance caused by production, for instance the construction work to build wells, the procession of tanker trucks and the pollution, but is also caused by the buyers' fear of the risks of groundwater

---

1 L. Muehlenbachs, E. Spiller and C. Timmins (2012), "Shale gas development and property values differences across drinking water sources", *Working paper series*, 18390, NBER

contamination. In the end, contrary to what supporters of exploitation compulsively repeat, if the American example was to be rapidly applied in France, the people supposedly living on top of a treasure would actually become poorer.

An Obsolete, Lawless Mining Code

Another point argued by the supporters of shale gas concerns the tax revenue that exploitation could generate. They remind us that France is going through a severe debt crisis and cannot do without public revenue. Once again, this argument is purposely simplified: in order for the State to be able to enjoy significant tax revenue, there need to be ground rules enabling the State to receive an important part of the benefits, should the resources be exploited. These legal rules are stipulated in the mining code.

However, today oil companies and their lobby groups exert pressure to rapidly obtain permits since the current legislation is extremely favourable to such companies, considering mining law remains essentially "production-oriented". In fact, when it was drafted in the 19th century, its main mission was to be "an instrument for public authorities to exploit subsurface resources to economic ends"[2]. But this should evolve, since French Minister for Ecology Delphine Batho aims to redraft the mining code. Companies are aware of that and have understood that a more modern mining code would be less favourable to them since it would take into account the environmental charter and establish new control over mining activities, with local populations and public authorities being more involved. All of this would bring about additional costs for companies, while negotiations with the various stakeholders could slow down the process of exploiting shale gas deposits.

Currently, mining law hardly takes environmental law into account – except by means of a few additions here and there –, although they should complement each other. Neither does the law provide for consultation, nor for inhabitants of production areas to be involved, although they are the most directly concerned if wells are drilled. Let us bear in mind that those who defend the necessity to produce shale gas are people who will not live close to areas of exploitation. However, as we have mentioned before, the people who reside close to the wells run the risk of becoming poorer because of the depreciation of their properties. In addition, we must consider the potential health hazards – which we will analyse below. Hence, it is necessary for nearby residents to be consulted with before well-drilling

---

2 A. Gossement (2011), *Mining law and environmental law: considerations for a reform of environmental evaluation, information and public participation* (*Droit minier et droit de l'environnement: éléments de réflexion pour une réforme relative à l'évaluation environnementale, à l'information et à la participation du public*) Report commissioned by N. Kosciusko-Morizet, 12 October.

licences can be issued. Finally, as Arnaud Gossement stated in a report commissioned by former French Minister for Ecology Nathalie Kosciusko-Morizet[3], mining law is a "lawyerless law". This should be remedied thanks to improvements in student training and academic research, to which the specialised skills of mining engineers need to be added, considering the highly sophisticated nature of the type of extraction that shale gas requires.

With the ground rules being established at the expense of local populations as well as of the environment – and, as a consequence, of future generations –, with those rules being all the more neglected given that there are few (if any) lawyers in the field, it is easier to understand why companies are in a hurry to obtain exploration permits. And it is easier to see why it is necessary to completely redraft the mining code before entering into any negotiation concerning the exploitation of our subsurface resources. Hence, we have to be patient and legally prepared so as to ensure that, should extractions happen in the future, France would be the big winner, as opposed to industrialists. Our new mining code should therefore provide for expensive royalties to be paid to the State and to regional authorities as well for as highly supervised production standards, in line with environ-mental law, and for very high fines in the case of an accident.

Certain oil tycoons will say that this type of regulations does not encourage companies to invest. Oil-producing African countries, which are amongst the poorest in the world in spite of thirty years of oil production, are all too familiar with

---

3   Idem.

such fine talk and are suffering its consequences. Nowadays, all the oil-producing countries that have become rich have at their disposal legislation that closely regulates company activity and is extremely favourable to the State. Conversely, the oil-producing countries whose rules favour companies are the poorest. That is the case in our former colonies which have inherited our mining code. That is why we must not hurry, since once a contract is signed with a company, our country is tied for the whole duration of the deposit's exploitation, that is to say for about thirty years.

Lies About the Need to "Explore not Exploit" French Subsoil

Since the case of shale gas exploitation has been closed, many companies claim the "right to explore the French subsoil if not to exploit it". According to their own arguments, they just want to undertake a quantifiable evaluation of resources, since the country ignores what reserves it possesses. Such generosity on the part of companies is surprising, for if they "explore without exploiting" the subsoil, they will lose money. But they know from experience that in the oil and gas industry, information is precious, and that to master it better than the State itself is a way to reap additional profit. Firstly, it tremendously accelerates the process of convincing public opinion. Secondly, the countries' shortage of information renders it easier for natural resources to be sold off.

If companies lobby for "the right to explore", it is because they know that it is precisely the best position from which to move to "exploitation" in the future.. It is a way to influence public opinion with repeated figures loaded with meaning. For instance, while no assessment has been made, Bruno Courme, Branch Director of Total Gas Shale Europe, still estimates that, exclusively for the Montelimar licence, reserves are equivalent to 10 to 20 times the annual consumption of gas in France, although has specified that at this stage, no figures are realistic[4]. This type of annoucements has a purpose: to influence public opinion. Indeed the formulated limits conceal a crucial message that is more emphasised than the rest: we own large reserves, therefore it is a mistake not to use them. In fact, the companies' strategy is working, since everyone seems to be convinced of France's shale gas potential, including the fiercest opponents to exploitation. Even former Prime Minister Michel Rocard estimates that "France is god-blessed" and that the country "has the potential to be to shale gas what Qatar is to oil". What bizarre enthusiasm when it is known that no serious assessment can evaluate shale gas reserves today.

In addition to this lack of information, companies have understood that the French State finds itself – as do many countries at the dawn of their oil-producing history – inexperienced and that only themselves can be called upon to reveal the potential of these resources. One is then faced

---

4 F. De Monicault (2011), "Shale gas: an unquantified resource in France" (« Gaz de schiste : une ressource non-quantifiée en France »), *Le figaro*, 22 April.

with a vicious circle, which many oil-producing countries have experienced: by calling on private companies to set up a resource assessment programme, many countries are only aware of the value of their subsoil through them. And it is based on the information given by their private experts that the terms are determined on which public natural resources will be sold to the companies themselves. Interests differ however, since companies may find it advantageous if the state receives as little money as possible, in order to monopolise more of the riches. But each of us must realise that if resources are sold off, the country has been stolen from.

Joseph Stiglitz, the Nobel Prize winner in Economic Sciences, wrote in his book entitled *Making Globalisation Work* that "it is the strategy of the oil, gas and mining companies to make sure that the government gets as little as possible – while, at the same time, helping the government find arguments for why it is good or even necessary for the government to receive so little". That is exactly what they did in Guiana, by luring the government with the prospects of job creations, financial gains and various investment projects, without broaching a crucial topic: the terms of the production-sharing contract. Thanks to certain media sources, we were even able to share the joy of the Guianese: "a taxi driver saw his takings increase by 20%", "packed house for a restaurant owner"... The same euphoria as had been experienced thirty years before in the Congo, in Gabon and in Cameroon, and probably the same disappointment in the end, when in twenty years' time everyone will understand that the billions from oil production have evaporated to fuel the profits of private companies at the expense of State revenues. Contrary to the United States, a gas – and oil-producing country whose history comprises quite a few legal battles disputes with mining companies, France has a very limited experience as a producer country. Without such qualifications as are necessary for a just evaluation of the risks or for an equitable sharing of wealth, the only weapon that we can use to establish a framework for production is the mining code.

There is nothing inane about our position. Is is obvious that, in France, some of the mining engineers employed in the public sector are as knowledgeable as their counterparts in the private sector. However the latter may find it advantageous to lie, whereas the former's advantage in telling the truth would be very limited (and often temporary). What results from this confrontation is a socially acceptable lie, that is to say a position that is different from collective interest but can still be justified by civil servants, a position which is favourable to the companies that have been able to produce this believable, albeit false, information. And it works, since what is striking about shale gas is the number of experts, politicians and citizens who have been blinded by the industrialists' arguments.

Speculation about Job Creation

The preferred argument of the industrialists in order to re-open the debate on shale gas is job creation. Many figures from the American example are quoted: 600,000 jobs have been said to be created. Certain consultancy firms, with strangely partial (both incomplete and biased) scientific reasoning, have begun making projections about the French case. In fact, according to Sia Conseil, one such firm, shale gas exploitation should create a minimum of 100,000 jobs by 2020[5]. In times of crisis, the figure is striking. Yet, unfortunately, it has willingly been exaggerated.

---

5 Press realease by SIA Conseil (2012), "Non-conventional gas: a minimum of 100,000 jobs to be created before 2020 according to SIA Conseil's estimations" (« Gaz non conventionnels: au minimum 100 000 emplois créés d'ici 2020 selon le scénario SIA Conseil. »), 19 September.

Firstly, this estimation only takes into account job creation, instead of taking into account the difference between job creation and job losses. In the lifetime of a typical well-shaft, the first years of exploitation are more demanding in terms of jobs than the following years. For instance, according to SIA Conseil's hypothesis, in the first three years, 13 people would be needed for a standard well to function whereas less than one person would be necessary (0.18, to be exact) for the next 20 years (after 20 to 25 years, the reserves that can be exploited by a single well would be exhausted). For the same well, the industry may create 13 jobs for three years, but then destroy more than 12 of them. In the end, in the long term, less than one job is created per well. This number coincides with the American numbers: over the past eight years, shale oil and shale gas exploitation is said to have created more than 600,000 jobs, directly and indirectly, for more than 500,000 wells, which amounts to a little more than one job (directly or indirectly) created per well.

Furthermore, the experts of SIA Conseil consider that the number of jobs increases proportionally to production, a calculation based on multiplying the job requirements of each well by the number of potential wells. However, thanks to economies of scale, any first-year economics student knows that employment does not increase proportionally to production. In the previous example, the 13 jobs created in the first well are either going to disappear or to be transferred to another well. Doubling production does not necessarily mean doubling staff. It appears as if, while taking it as axiomatic that producing one car demands three workers, one considered that the two million cars that are produced annually were to result in the creation of six million jobs. It is absurd.

Besides, an article published in the scientific journal *Energy Economics*[6] shows that a strong increase in gas production only results in a limited increase in job creation and salaries. According to the article, for each million dollar made, gas production only creates 2,35 jobs! The author also reminds us that job creation had been overestimated before exploitation started. Indeed, gas production, as all extractive industries, demands little manpower, with most needs concentrated in the early stages of the production cycle.

All hydrocarbon specialists know this: once the well has been installed, gas production demands little effort for the next twenty years. So little in fact that it is referred to as « gas rents". Indeed, among the biggest gas-producing countries, neither Norway nor Russia has managed to create as many jobs as the United States, in such little time. The Americans' secret advantage is solely due to intensive drilling in exploited areas, since to produce jobs continuously, drilling has to be permanent. Figures prove it: there are about one million active oil and gas wells in the United States today, and over the past few years, Americans have drilled more than 40,000 wells annually. The development of shale gas in the United States thus rather resembles a true "gold rush", wild, irrational, than optimal management of resources,

---

6   J.G. Weber (2012), "The effects of a natural gas boom on employment and income in Colorado, Texas, and Wyoming", *Energy Economics*, n°34, p.1580-1588

even without considering health and environmental risks. Yet, it is that model that some are trying to import to France.

In fact, when viewing figures about certain gas-producing areas in the United States, one better understands why companies are in such a hurry to exploit French reserves: the value generated by production is unrelated to economic benefits in terms of employment. For instance, in 2007 in Fayetteville (Arkansas), gas production rose up to 586 million dollars yet only demanded the creation of 1377 jobs as against the 9533 which were initially planned for.

The Lie of a Cheaper Gas Bill

Many industrialists and consultants promise that, if we exploit shale gas, the gas bills of French households will become cheaper. Based on the case of the United States and on the previsions of the American consultancy firm IHS[7], which show how non-conventional gas exploration could enable each American household to save 926 dollars a year, some put forward the argument that the energy bill would be lower for French households too. This has been a major argument to re-open the debate on shale gas exploitation, especially when a survey carried out by the French polling company CSA on behalf of the national energy ombudsman reveals that 80% of the French population say that they feel concerned about energy bills.

---

7   IHS Global Insight (2011), "The Economic and Employment Contributions of Natural Gas in the United States", December.

But yet again, shale gas supporters willingly simplify too much, strictly applying the American experience to France without taking into account the disparities between the two countries, on the level of how the gas market works as well as regarding the legal and institutional specificities in each country.

At global level, there are three types of gas markets which work according to different rules: the American market, the European market and the Asian market. We will focus on the differences between the American gas market and the European gas market, since they are essential to an understanding of why French bills are not going to become cheaper.

The American gas market is a spot market, the price of which depends on the evolution of supply and demand on the short term. It is a flexible market in which prices can be affected by rapid, sometimes important, fluctuations. Thanks to the "incredible" growth of shale gas drilling in the United States, gas supply has greatly increased on the market, at a time when demand has been decreasing because of the economic crisis. This resulted in an immediate fall in spot prices for gas, down to the level of 3 dollars per million BTU[8] versus 8 dollars in 2010.

Besides, when gas price curves in Europe and the United States are compared, they appear to have been almost identical until 2010. Then, gas prices fell in the United States (thanks to shale gas production) and rose slightly in Europe, with a price difference of about 7$. Indeed, this is the

---

8   British Thermal Units (BTU) is the unit used to measure the value of gas determined by its energy potential measured in BTU.

favourite argument of most pro-shale gas economists. Today, those who are used to scrutinizing the summary indexes of financial markets, without truly knowing the market value of listed companies, have started scrutinizing the price curves of American gas, without wondering whether this price is valid considering the evolution of the actual costs sustained by exploiting companies.

Indeed if the market price is not sustainable, it means that there is a bubble, that is to say a gap between prices and reality, which would inevitably be followed by a brutal adjustment – the bursting of the bubble – the disastrous consequences of which on the economy are known to everyone.

Actually, there already is a debate on whether to keep gas prices durably low in the United States. New-York based Ben Dell from Bernstein Research considers that to cover the total cost of research, development and the exploitation of shale gas wells, gas needs to cost 7.50\$ to 8\$ per million BTU[9], which almost amounts to the European price! On this matter, several gas company Presidents such as Aubrey McClendon from Chesapeake Energy Corp deem the current price to be unsustainable[10] and already mention a potential price bubble. Indeed, even though the growth of shale drillings is impressive in the United States, it cannot

---

9   See J. Dizard (2010), "The true cost of shale gas production", *Financial Times*, 7 March.

10   See R. Bell et O. Rusetsky (2012), "Shale gas: should we thank Hollande?" (« Gaz de schiste : faut-il remercier Hollande ? »), *La tribune*, 23 October.

durably maintain prices lower than the costs of extraction, or else shale gas exploitation will no longer be profitable and will therefore be abandoned, which eventually will result in supplies being reduced and prices going up again (the bubble then bursting). It is highly likely that these estimations regarding American gas prices will come true, since they are eventually bound to follow the same route as European prices.

Yet, even without considering the bubble effect, the American experience cannot be duplicated in France, since the European gas market works differently. In Europe, the gas market is more rigid and based on long-term contracts, signed for 10 to 30 years, with supplier countries. Those contracts are unique in that they index gas prices to oil prices. The question is to find out if, on a more rigid market, shale gas exploitation would lead to lower costs (or a bubble) as in the United States?

That is far from being certain, for if shale gas is cheaper than imported gas, in the end gas prices on the market always fall in to line with the highest price. It is an old principle which dates back to English economist David Ricardo, who, thanks to the concept of differential rent, showed how, when agricultural land was unevenly fertile, the price of wheat was determined on the basis of the least fertile land – or else farmers would have had no interest in producing that wheat. The important thing to remember in Ricardo's concept is that, in a context of strong demand, when production costs for the same goods vary, the cost of those goods always depends on the highest production cost, because otherwise parts of the goods would not make a profit and there would be a shortage.

The same exact principle applies to gas prices in France, where the State-regulated tariff takes into account the different production costs and must allow for complete coverage of all those costs (supply, transportation, storage and marketing) for the most expensive sorts of gas, to prevent shortages. Except if some of the gas distribution companies agree to sell at a loss – which is forbidden by law –, or if the State agrees to subsidise imported gas prices so as to bring them into line with supposedly cheaper shale gas costs – which is unlikely. In that case, even with a more economical production of shale gas, the State-imposed tariff will still be a price that can cover the costs of imported gas. In fact, some thought that with the 2007 liberalisation, prices would fall; yet, in the end they have always remained close to the regulated tariff for the same reasons[11].

It is true that some will continue to argue that prices could become lower in Europe, since long-term contracts are not exclusively indexed to oil prices any more and since they occupy a bigger share of the spot market (around 46% in France). But even supposing that spot prices should decrease with shale gas production as was the case in the United States, the share that depends on oil prices – those prices being on a structural upward trend since 2004 – will act as a stabiliser. Eventually, contrary to the American gas market, the more rigid European gas market erases short-term movements, and (until the bubble explodes) temporarily prevents a decrease in gas prices.

---

11   With decreases in differentials to a maximum of 5% under certain restrictive conditions regarding consumption.

If industrialists put forward the argument of cheaper gas bills, as though they worried more about the well-being of French households than about their own profits, it is because they know perfectly well that the rigidity of the European market can allow them to make huge profit margins, superior to those of their American counterparts. Indeed, by producing rather cheaply-extracted gas and later selling for a higher price (that of imported gas), companies will make enormous profits without any significant positive impact on consumer bills.

The Myth of Renewed Competitiveness because of Shale Gas

Another argument put forth by certain politicians, economists and foundations of all kinds is that of the increased industrial competitiveness which would derive from shale gas exploitation. There seems to be a consensus in this debate, and even the Gallois Report advocates that research on shale gas exploitation techniques should be boosted.

Some economists have even calculated how big the American competitive advantage is and how threatening it could become to the European industry as a result. Patrick Artus, Director of Economic Research for the French investment bank Natixis, explains in *Flash Economie* that the United States have exploited their shale gas, not for the purposes of gas exportation but to provide their industry with a durable competitive advantage. He adds that Europeans must become aware of the threat that this poses to their industries, all the more so since the shale-gas based competitive advantage of the United States adds to the one induced by labour costs[12]. In another issue of *Flash Economie,* Patrick Artus even proposes to calculate the drop in natural gas prices in terms of the equivalent drop in American industrial wages, compared with Europe. According to the article, this would be equivalent to a 6% drop in labour costs[13].

But Patrick Artus's analysis can be criticised since it is based on the premise that shale gas prices would durably be kept low in the United States. Yet, as explained above, prices are bound to rise (at best, the situation is highly uncertain and does not allow for low gas prices to be used as a basic premise), in which case Patrick Artus's analyses on the competitive advantage of the American industry are debunked. Moreover, in the case of France, we have also shown that gas prices would not fall, which plainly and simply cancels any possible impacts on the French industry.

Besides, even without taking into account the long-term contracts mentioned in the previous chapter, in Europe, extraction costs may be higher than gas market prices, notably because of a lack of infrastructure. In that

---

12   P. Artus (2012), "Shale gas in the United States: Europeans must take the threat to their industries seriously" (« Gaz de schiste aux États-Unis : les Européens doivent prendre au sérieux la menace sur leur industrie »), *Flash économie*, N°637, 26 September

13   P. Artus (2012), "The weight of the natural-gas-based American competitive advantage" (« La taille de l'avantage compétitif des États-Unis dû au gaz naturel »), *Flash économie*, N°151, 17 February.

case, there can be no economic gains derived from gas extraction: the energy bill would only increase and the industry would become less competitive. This is precisely one of the paradoxes of the shale gas question: if extraction is undertaken under environmentally friendly conditions, then extraction costs increase and gas market prices are less likely to fall.

We must also refocus the debate on the true issues that the French industry is faced with. Today, the lack of competitiveness in France is rather a problem of quality than of cost. For instance, a Peugeot car costs less than a Volkswagen car. In terms of price competitiveness, the Peugeot car has an advantage, and if competitiveness was only price-based, everyone would choose to buy it to the detriment of the Volkswagen car. However, as facts show, Peugeot sells less cars than Volkswagen. Indeed the true problem of our industry's competitiveness lies more in the quality of its production and in its specialisation than in the price advantage.

Despite of all this, CEOs (and shareholders) will always defend the idea that lowering costs is the only solution, since, as everyone knows, it is simpler to make additional profits by putting pressure on employees rather than by thinking of means to make better-quality products. The myth of dropping oil prices thanks to a domino effectThose in favour of exploitation assert that the substantial rise in oil supply due to the production of shale oil, as well as the competition between energies (oil replaced by shale gas in the industry) should, through a domino effect, result in lower oil prices. According to an Alphavalue study, they could even be down to 50$ by 2015[14]. This is an argument of great consequence when it is known that rising oil prices hurt our trade balance every year, and that they directly influence French people's purchasing power via oil costs.

Yet, once again, the argument does not hold. At best, it can be said that this projection could be true *if all other things were equal*, that is to say in a fossilised world. As economist Jacques Généreux explains, such a projection is of the following type: "at a specific place, at a specific time, if nothing moves in the universe other than variable X, it should result in such and such variation of variables Y or Z [15]". Thinking that oil prices could decrease durably to 50$ is a true misunderstanding of the way the oil market works.

Firstly, one must acknowledge the existence of a cartel in the oil market: the Organisation of the Petroleum Exporting Countries (OPEC) indeed represents 40% of global production. In fact, the *raison d'être* of OPEC is to influence oil prices while they adjust their own production quotas in order to put pressure on prices. Currently, Gulf countries (the main oil producers in OPEC) need to run enormous budget surpluses since, with "the Arab spring", they have increased social spendings. Saudi Arabia is said to have added 130 billion dollars in spendings for education, health and social affairs. In that context, the

---

14   A. Andlauer, Financial analysis company Alphavalue, (2012), "Towards 50 dollar oil in 2015?" (« Vers un pétrole à 50 dollars en 2015 ? », The Energy Chain (La chaine de l'énergie), *L'expansion*, 5 October.

15   J. Généreux (2005), *The true laws of the Economy* (*Les vraies lois de l'économie*), éd. Points, p. 44

The mirage of the shale gas

trade balance of Gulf countries could not durably bear fifty-dollar oil. Indeed many OPEC countries claim that they need prices to be close to 100$ to cover their economic and social expenditures. Can we thus seriously think that OPEC countries would let the price of oil drop to 50$ without reacting? The answer is self-evident: if shale gas and shale oil exploitation resulted in a decrease in oil prices, the organisation would lower their production quotas to make prices rise again.

Secondly, oil is not a standard product and its production costs vary according to where it is extracted. Whereas in a standard industry, manufacturing costs tend to fall proportionally to production – which automatically leads to lower prices –, in the oil industry, production costs (extraction costs) rise in ratio to quantities produced, since oil companies develop oilfields in increasingly inaccessible areas. However, to exploit these oilfields where extraction is expensive, companies need oil prices to be high enough, so that they can make a profit (*i.e.* prices superior to extraction costs). Today, with oil prices higher than 110 dollars, oil that is drilled in very deep water (as in Guiana) becomes profitable, but an increase in supply could not bring prices lower than the extraction costs for this deep-water oil, or else it would not be profitable anymore. It is clear that even if shale oil extraction techniques were to be perfected, that even if their extraction costs were to become lower, at global level, oil prices would not decrease. Indeed if they came to decrease, then quite a few sorts of oil (very deep-water oil, Arctic oil) would not be profitable anymore, which would result in supplies being reduced and prices going up again.

The trend increase in oil extraction costs therefore acts as a "stabiliser" of its price.

In the end, when taking into account the specificities of the oil market, the argument according to which shale gas exploitation would lower oil prices does not hold. In fact, in 2012, in spite of the substantial rise in shale gas and shale oil production in the United States over the past few years, the average Brent crude oil price reached 111$, beating its personal record for the fourth year in a row.

The Lack of Studies on the Impact on People's Health

The current debate on shale gas exploitation has glossed over an important factor: its impact on the health of populations residing near exploitation areas. A report by the National Institute for Public Health commissioned by the Quebec Minister for Health[16] draws a few interesting conclusions from the American example.

The report indicates that "the information thus obtained has rendered it possible to partially support the hypothesis of a causal relation between shale gas exploitation and certain health effects". Primarily though, the report points out several times the lack of information and of studies on the topic: "the

---

16   Institut national de santé du Quebec (2010), "The State of scientific knowledge on the relations between shale gas-related activities and public health", Preliminary Report, (« état des connaissances sur la relation entre les activités liées au gaz de schiste et la santé publique », *Rapport Préliminaire*), Direction de la santé environnementale et de la toxicologie, November.

lack of information essential to this evaluation must be noted, notably concerning the techniques that were employed, the substances that were used as well as the quantity of pollutants that were emitted", or "to this day, there does not exist an in-depth study of the consequences on health of shale gas exploitation and water", or again "the knowledge we have on the quality of the water affected by shale gas exploitation is incomplete, only rare areas of exploitation are subjected to surveillance regarding water contamination".

The report also notes the indirect nuisance as a result of traffic, noise, the emission of harmful particles or drilling-related vibrations. If France follows the same drilling rhythm as the United States, the neighbouring populations will constantly endure this nuisance, without mentioning those directly linked to hydraulic fracturing.

On that note, another report by the University of Colorado[17], published in 2008, states that: "judging by the available evidence, oil and gas exploration activities are likely to have severe effects on people's health. In spite of this possibility, oil and gas industries have failed to take reasonable measures to protect the families and communities in question". Lastly, a scientific article published in 2012 by researchers from the University of Colorado[18] shows that living within a half-mile

---

17   R Witter *et al.* (2008), *Potential Exposure Relate Human Health Effects of Oil and Gas Development: A Literature review (2003-2008)*, Colorado School of Public Health, University of Colorado Denver, April.

18   L. M. Mc Kenzie *et al* (2012), "Human Health risk assessment of air emissions from development of unconventional natural gas resources", *Science of the total environment*, Volume 424, p 79-87.

radius (805 meters) around a well increases the risks of developing a cancer, because of the toxic discharges in the air.

The conclusions of these various reports are irrevocable. First because they show, as explained above, the lack of symmetrical information between public instances and companies, but mostly because they confirm the absence of real studies before, or even during the development of resources. Industrialists and their unofficial lobby groups often militate for a looser precautionary principle, but an in-depth analysis of the American case shows that, in shale gas production, no precautionary principle has been followed, whether to protect people's health or the environment. In spite of all this, currently, in Fance, it is that very model that some call "miraculous".

The Myth of Energy Independence

Those in favour of exploitation constantly assert this position: shale gas and shale oil would enable France to reach energy independence. In fact, this will soon be the case for the United States. It is confirmed in a report by the International Energy Agency (IEA) which announces that the United States should become the world-leading country in oil production in 2020 and a net exporter around 2030[19].

But the IEA's conclusions are open to criticism and it is important for everyone to understand how the agency's projections are made. First of all, IEA economists have access to a large amount of data to build their model: oil production, demand, economic growth, etc. This data is considered as conventionally-evolving parameters, which means that the main hypothesis is that the current state of

---

19   IEA (2012), *World Energy Outlook* (WEO 2012)

things will continue indefinitely. Consequently, according to the IEA, the world in 2030 is nothing but the conventional evolution of today's world (*all things being otherwise equal,* or close). This means that in the current state of things, the United States will be the leading oil-producing country in 2020 if they continue to drill at the same speed for the next ten years – which is nothing short of an average of 40,000 new oil shafts a year – and that if they maintain this insane rhythm for twenty years, they will be able to achieve energy independence.

If they followed this model, the United States would therefore reach 2030 with more than 1.7 million shafts and would be an "isolated energy island" surrounded with a passive world defined as steady data. But in the real world, such a development of American shale oil and gas production would bring up many related questions: could the American territory bear such numerous drillings? Would the nearby populations let producers drill for ever? Would OPEC countries and other gas producers stand by and watch as American production becomes more powerful? Would water resources be sufficient for all wells? IEA models implicitly answer "yes". Unfortunately, human beings, countries and the world are not mere parameters in a series of equations and IEA projections actually only consider one situation amongst so many potential others. In reality, the IEA is much more likely to be wrong than right, but the agency leaves this information out.

What is more, the IEA has already made numerous mistakes. For instance, in 2000, the Agency predicted that the price of a barrel of oil would reach 21$ in 2010 and 28$

in 2020 on average[20]. Yet, the average price was 111$ in 2012, five times more than predicted! The explanation for this error is simple: the IEA has seen the world of 2010 and 2020 as a conventional evolution of the world of 2000. IEA models had therefore not integrated the strong growth of emerging countries, which partly accounts for the discrepancy between oil prices. Neither could they predict the economic crises, nor the Arab spring.

None of this would matter, if those results did not impact on the life on millions of people. Some countries have paid a high price for the mistaken projections of the IEA. The Congo is one example, since, as many poor oil-producing countries, the country sells its oil in advance to major companies (Total, BP, etc.) It is difficult for the Congo to sell its oil in advance when the price varies every day on the markets. This is when IEA projections come into play.

Frequently, the value of the anticipated sale is the result of an arbitrage between spot market prices (the current cost of the barrel) at the time of negotiation, and IEA projections (in which "haircuts" [discounts] differ less according to quality and purchased quantities). In 2004, because of the strong growth of emerging countries, which the IEA had not taken into account in its model, the Brent crude oil price reached 44$ during the summer. This raised a question in the negotiations between the Congo and oil companies: was the discrepancy in oil prices to be explained by long-term changes in the structure of the market (with the arrival of emerging countries) or by short-term instability? Today,

---

20   IEA (2000), *World Energy Outlook* (WEO 2000)

everyone knows the answer: it was the beginning of a rising trend for oil prices. But at that time, the only trustworthy point of comparison was the projection models of the IEA and the experts' explanations (which were generally based on IEA conclusions). The Congo thus sold its oil in 2004 for the price of 20$ (the price set by the IEA, minus several "haircuts"). In fact, it turned out that the average cost of a barrel in the year 2004 was 38$, which represented a loss of 18$ per barrel for the Congo. In total, that amounts to a shortfall of at least 500 million dollars only for 2004 – which is equivalent to twenty times the spendings for development aid for that same year!

The Congo is a typical example of the negative effects on the population that can derive from the IEA's mistakes. However, paradoxically, despite the agency's inability to question its own errors and despite its use of the same methods that inevitably lead to the same mistakes, the IEA enjoys a high degree of credibility in the eyes of politicians and economists. Today, when the agency asserts that the United States will become the leading oil-producing country in 2020 and a net exporter in 2030, it legitimises shale gas production as an economic treasure – far beyond anyone's expectations – and turns the "gold rush" into a model energy policy. The supporters of exploitation did not fail to spread this "false" good news.

THE MYTH OF THE GLOBAL GEOPOLITICAL UPHEAVAL

Behind shale gas production lies a supposed spectacular reshuffling of the global geopolitical pack. The supporters of exploitation are adamant: in 20 years from now, the United States will be independent in terms of energy and will not rely on oil and gas imports from Gulf countries anymore. Some experts even argue that North America could replace Saudi Arabia as the swing supplier (a producer able to stand in for any other producers/exporters, should they be unable to produce) by 2020. Others even predict the end of OPEC. This is the core argument of a paper by Amy Myers Jaffe, which explains how by 2020 the global centre of gravity in terms of energy supply will move from the Middle East to the United States[21].

---

21   A. M. Jaffe (2011), "Oil: OPEC is finished" (« Pétrole : l'OPEP est fini »), *Slate*, 19 August.

Again, the arguments put forth by shale gas lobbyists display severe lack of judgment. Indeed similar geopolitical situations have occurred before in oil history. In the 1970s, at the time of the oil crises, the United States and Europe, severely hit by the rise in oil prices, encouraged their oil companies to launch programmes of exploration and production in countries outside of OPEC. This was the case for Elf in particular, the French company which mainly developed its production in Africa. The aim was to diversify sources of supply and ultimately to weaken the market power of OPEC.

At global level, oil supply began to increase while the OPEC share in it started to decline, from 55% in 1973 to less than 30% in 1985. Many thought that they were witness to a major geopolitical upheaval. Some already predicted the death of the organisation. However, the development of oil in non-OPEC countries did not radically change the geopolitical balance. Indeed, what has always given OPEC a major geopolitical role on the global stage is the fact that it is the sole organisation that can resort to an excess production capacity, should important tensions arise on the market – wars, soaring demand, etc. –, whereas non-OPEC producting countries have always produced to full capacity and do not have any surplus production that they could directly resort to.

Currently, the development of shale oil in the United States and Canada has led certain experts to the conclusion that North America could replace OPEC in that role by 2020. But this argument is too hastily put forth, since in order to become a swing supplier, most than anything else, a country needs the political will to do so. This includes the State's agreeing to limit its oil exports by means of quota-based production, which leaves the surplus production available for use if a problem arises. For instance, in 2012, OPEC produced 30 million barrels a day while its estimated production capacity was 35,45 million barrels a day. The organisation thus willingly limits its production.

Therefore, the role of swing supplier has more to do with political will than oil production levels. Also, the manner that shale gas production has developed over the past years in the United States does not seem in any way like the concerted political management of a natural resource. Under those conditions, chances are that, even if the United States increases shale gas and shale oil production, the country will not become the global centre of gravity in terms of energy, since if any geopolitical problem involving an oil-producing country arises, the international community will to turn to OPEC countries, thus underlining their still crucial role in global energy challenges.

DENIAL OF THE DEBATE ON SHALE GAS AND GO FOR ENERGY TRANSITION

Since the United States refused to sign the Kyoto Protocol, the entire world has been aware that American political choices grant environmental issues but a minor interest. The Kyoto agreements were certainly far from perfect but they bore a strong symbolical value: for the first time, all countries decided to work as a team for the environment, more precisely for the climate. It is clear that Kyoto agreements are limiting. They force our societies to change without providing us with better living standards; more than anything else they are indeed a gift to future generations.

Evidently, the richest countries were asked to make a greater effort. Indeed, the Protocol proposed to reduce greenhouse gas emissions by industrialised countries – by 7% in the United States, as against 8% for Europe and 6% for Japan – without imposing any restrictions on developing countries. But it makes complete sense when one knows that in 2004, an American citizen emitted 20,37 tons of carbon dioxyde on average, as against 3,83 for the average Chinese et 0,05 for the average Malian.

In addition, this distribution of effort is logical for two reasons: the biggest polluter countries are also the richest, and since they are rich, they are best able to make an effort. Today, G8 countries only represent 13% of the global population but the share of their GDP in the global GDP is as high as 56%. In terms of the ecological footprint, if the 7 billion people on the planet lived as Americans do, we would need 5 planets – 3 if they lived as French people do. Based on these figures, it seems evident that the effort should be made first and foremost by the richest countries.

Nonetheless, the United States decided not to take part in this effort since the country estimated that the costs inflicted on the American economy were greater than future benefits. It is a selfish choice for two main reasons. Firstly, because as the leading polluters and the major contributors to global warming, the United States create negative externalities that affect the whole planet. But their estimation regarding cost being greater than benefits is correct, for in most cases – except for the fact that parts of Manhattan run the risk of being underwater in the future – the most violent impact of climate change will hurt the most vulnerable populations of the globe, those for whom seasons and climate are important for farming, animal-breeding or fishing. It is estimated that a rise of 4°C in temperature would result in more than a billion climate refugees[22].

---

22   Source: Policy exchange (2011).

Secondly, as the first world power, the United States sends a very negative signal to the rest of the world as to how to deal with environmental issues. What can be expected of other countries if the first world power considers the environment as a second-rate question? In fact, that signal has been received and in 2011, Russia, Japan and Canada warned that they would not be involved in 2010 in a "second Kyoto". The United States also confirmed that the country would not change its position.

The Kyoto agreements are losing substance, while a World Bank report[23], issued in november 2012, sends out an alarm signal regarding global warming and calls for "concerted, rapid international action" as well as a more "intelligent" use of energy and natural resources[24]. Yet the United States does the exact opposite with shale gas production, and still it is based on that example that such production is being promoted in France.

Even worse, some people use global warming as a selling point: shale gas supposedly emits less greenhouse gas than other energies. Lobby groups of biofuel producers already put forth similar arguments[25] in the past. Yet they did not take into account the environmental costs of production.

---

23   World Bank (2012), *4°C: Turn down the heat: Why a 4°c warmer world must be avoided*, November.

24   Lemonde.fr with AFP (2012), "The World bank fears cataclysm if global warming rises by 4°C" (« La banque mondiale redoute le cataclysme d'un réchauffement climatique de 4°C »), 19 November.

25   See J. Ziegler (2011), *Massive Destruction (Destruction Massive)*, Paris: Seuil, p. 251-254.

Similarly, the highly energy-consuming production of shale gas is one of the factors that make it unattractive in terms of climate[26].

Lastly, the large quantities of water that are necessary for drilling and hydraulic fracturing must not be ignored. As IFP (Institut français du pétrole, the French oil institute) geologist Roland Vially recalls: "for each well drilled, the quantity of water used is around 10,000 to 15,000 m^3 (in comparison, the city of Paris consumes 550,000 m^3 of drinkable water per day)". A report by the American EPA (Environmental Protection Agency) estimates that each year in the United States, the quantity of water used for hydraulic fracturing is as high as the annual consumption of 80 cities of 50,000 inhabitants each[27]. Roland Vially, in an interview on the IFP website, reminds us that "this industrial use of water must not conflict with water supply for human consumption or agriculture", although unfortunately, we can already witness the opposite.

Everywhere in the world, populations of adults and children suffer from water shortage. In 2009, the UNESCO report entitled "Water in a changing world" brought up a few figures that each of us must bear in mind. First of all,

---

26   B. Schepper, L. Handal and P. Herbert (2011), "Shale gas: a profitable environment-friendly solution for Quebec?" (« Gaz de schiste : une filière écologique et profitable pour le Québec ? »), *Note Socio-économique*, IRIS (Institut de Recherche et d'Informations Socio-économiques), February.

27   EPA (2011), *Draft Plan to Study the Potential Impacts of Hydraulic Fracturing on Drinking Water Resources*, Office of Research and Development U.S Environmental Protection Agency Washington, D.C

the report mentions that "competition for water exists on all levels and that it is expected to rise with demand for water in almost every country". If shale gas is developed in Europe on a large scale, this competition will be intensified as well as the shortages that it will entail for certain populations. Today, almost a tenth of global deaths could be avoided thanks to better water supply, waste water treatment, hygiene and water resource management. Each year, 1.4 million children die of diarrhoeal diseases which could be prevented. Undernutrition is an underlying cause of 53% of all deaths among children under five, and the lack of access to sufficient food is partly linked to bad water resource management[28].

---

28   UNESCO (2009), *Water in a changing world/ L'eau dans un monde qui change*, third United Nations World Water Development Report.

Let's Close the Debate on Shale Gas and Go for Energy Transition

The haste with which industrialists want to exploit shale gas in France is understandable. We now know that the value of "hundreds of millions of dollars" in production is disconnected from job creation; that the production-oriented mining code, and the lack of lawyers, are extremely favourable to companies since they impose very few limits in terms of the environment and of taxes; that when taking into account the European gas market, more rigid that the American one, shale gas production – thanks to the difference in production costs when compared to imported gas – would allow companies to make additional profits without even lowering the gas bills of consumers.

Despite all this, some will continue to put forth the American experience as an example to follow. We know that it rather resembles a "wild gold rush" than the concerted handling of a country's energy legacy, and everyone must be aware that if we model our economic results after those of the United States, then we will have to drill more than 90,000 wells in the coming years, which would result in nuisances and health hazards for nearby populations. The latter have already expressed their dissent on this issue, as has the rest of France (according to an IFOP poll, 72% of the population demand "the permanent ban on exploration and exploitation of these non-conventional hydrocarbons[29]"). However we know that those who push for shale gas production do not live in potential exploitation areas and that, despite speeches on collective interest, they will seize most of the riches without having to suffer any of the negative effects of drilling (pollution risks, etc.).

Nonetheless, contrary to what lobbyists argue, not using shale gas is relevant in terms of the French economy. Indeed, those resources are not lost: they remain in our subsoil. And, considering that gas prices, as oil prices, are on a structural upward trend, if in ten years, the government decides to extract shale gas, its value on the market, and its profitability, will be all the more important. As far as extraction techniques are concerned, they will have improved. In the end, keeping the gas underground is a bit like holding savings with a very high interest rate. Mostly, it leaves the possibility open for future generations to use it we fail to achieve the energy transition.

Today, the government seems to take a chance on the energy transition. And why not? It is in line with European objectives to reduce greenhouse gas emissions by 20%,

---

29   WWF poll carried out by IFOP, 11 September 2012.

increase energy efficiency by 20% and raise the share of renewable energies in production to 20%. It is an ambitious project, but to some pople, Europe's exemplariness is pointless. On the contrary, by imposing extra weight on Europe, this project would compromise the Union's growth and competitivity. I do not share that opinion. It may be true that the various world climate conferences have not led to a consensus to improve or supervise our patterns of production, but without Europe, one pattern would already be in use: the mere denial of global warming. The debate must thus continue, in the hope that one day it may have a ripple effect on other countries.

For all these reasons, before blindly wanting to follow the American example in shale gas production, we must depoliticise the debate and get to know the issues at stake that reach further than the mere production of these types of gas. It is true that it would be simpler for politicians –but also for the citizens who are responsible for bringing them to power- to turn a deaf ear or to make do with "mini-measures" regarding the environment, than to take wide-ranging measures, however essential to mankind these may be. Yet, everyone must realise that we will have no second chance, since unfortunately, until now, we only know one planet we can live on -Earth.

Table of Contents

Best sellers Max Milo Editions

Hitler's banker, Jean-François Bouchard

Confessions of a forger, Éric Piedoie Le Tiec

The Koran and the flesh, Ludovic-Mohamed Zahed

Governing by fake news, Jacques Baud

Governing by chaos, Collectif

A political history of food, Paul Ariès

Mad in U.S.A.: The ravages of the "American model",
Michel Desmurget

Mondial soccer club geopolitics, Kévin Veyssière

Putin: Game master?, Jacques Braud

Treatise on the three impostors: Moses, Jesus, Muhammad,
The Spirit of Spinoza

TV Lobotomy, Michel Desmurget